The Healthy Protein KITCHEN

The Healthy Protein KITCHEN

*Feel-good food for
happy and healthy eating*

LOVE FOOD™

This edition published by Parragon Books Ltd in 2017
LOVE FOOD is an imprint of Parragon Books Ltd

Parragon Books Ltd
Chartist House
15–17 Trim Street
Bath BA1 1HA, UK
www.parragon.com/lovefood

ISBN 978–1–4748–3798–9

Printed in China

New recipes by Joy Skipper
Introduction by Judith Wills
Cover and new recipe photography by Tony Briscoe
Home economy by Sian Davies

NOTES FOR THE READER

This book uses both metric and imperial measurements. Follow the same units of measurement throughout; do not mix metric and imperial. All spoon measurements are level: teaspoons are assumed to be 5 ml, and tablespoons are assumed to be 15 ml. Unless otherwise stated, milk is assumed to be full fat, eggs and individual fruits and vegetables are medium, pepper is freshly ground black pepper and salt is table salt. A pinch of salt is calculated as $1/16$ of a teaspoon. Unless otherwise stated, all root vegetables should be peeled prior to using.

The times given are an approximate guide only. Preparation times differ according to the techniques used by different people and the cooking times may also vary from those given. Please note that any ingredients stated as being optional are not included in the nutritional values provided. The nutritional values given are approximate and provided as a guideline only, they do not account for individual cooks, scales and portion sizes. The nutritional values provided are per serving or per item.

While the publisher of the book and the original author(s) of the recipes and other text have made all reasonable efforts to ensure that the information contained in this book is accurate and up to date at the time of publication, anyone reading this book should note the following important points: –
* Medical and pharmaceutical knowledge is constantly changing and the author(s) and the publisher cannot and do not guarantee the accuracy or appropriateness of the contents of this book;
* In any event, this book is not intended to be, and should not be relied upon, as a substitute for appropriate, tailored professional advice. Both the author(s) and the publisher strongly recommend that a doctor or other healthcare professional is consulted before embarking on major dietary changes;
* For the reasons set out above, and to the fullest extent permitted by law, the author(s) and publisher: (i) cannot and do not accept any legal duty of care or responsibility in relation to the accuracy or appropriateness of the contents of this book, even where expressed as 'advice' or using other words to this effect; and (ii) disclaim any liability, loss, damage or risk that may be claimed or incurred as a consequence – directly or indirectly – of the use and/or application of any of the contents of this book.

CONTENTS

WHAT IS PROTEIN?

Protein is one of the major nutrients our bodies need for health, growth and normal functioning, and we need to consume it regularly. It is a component of many foods but it doesn't always take the same form. It consists of combinations of amino acids – often called protein's 'building blocks' – which are vital for every metabolic process in our bodies and make up a large proportion of our cells, muscles and tissue. Protein-containing foods vary in the amount and type of these amino acids that they contain.

Protein is essential for building, maintaining and repairing cells and for the actual structure of cells. It also helps protect us from viral and bacterial infections and boosts the immune system; acts as a co-ordinator between various body processes; helps with body movement; and transports atoms and molecules around the body. Surplus protein can also be converted into energy (calories).

Our total protein needs may alter according to our circumstances. Body weight is perhaps the most important factor – adults need around 0.75g of protein a day per kg of their weight. Pregnant and breast-feeding women also need more protein than average, while factors such as age and activity levels may alter our optimum intake.

Most adults in the UK, USA and Australia for example do eat enough protein, according to official figures, but protein deficiency and malnutrition throughout the world is common. High activity levels increase protein needs by up to 50% and some research shows that older people may need around 25% more protein than younger adults.

While vegetarians don't need more protein than anyone else, they need to get a good daily variety of protein-containing foods so they get all the essential amino acids.

Our recipes include a balanced mix of natural protein types including vegetable, meat, fish and dairy proteins. The vegetable-based recipes aren't necessarily strictly vegetarian or vegan so do check the ingredients list.

Your protein intake can be improved by making good choices at any meal of the day. Healthy breakfasts, lunches, snacks, dinners and desserts that are higher in protein than perhaps your usual choices can help to increase your protein levels.

VEGETABLE-BASED PROTEINS

Vegetable-based protein sources are an excellent choice and offer a range of health and nutritional benefits. When people think of 'protein' foods they often think of animal sources such as meat and fish. But it is not difficult to get your daily requirements of protein by choosing more – or even all – from the wide range of vegetable-based foods. These include pulses such as fresh and dried beans, peas and lentils; nuts, and seeds. Many other types of vegetables are good or useful sources of protein.

Humans need 20 different types of amino acids. The body can manufacture 11 of these but the other 9 are called essential (or indispensible) because they must come from the diet. Individual foods that do contain all of the essential amino acids are called 'complete proteins'.

Few individual vegetable-based protein foods are classified as 'complete proteins' but all vegetable sources do contain a mix of some or most of the essential amino acids. If you eat a good variety of vegetable protein sources every day, then it is unlikely that you will go short. Soya beans, quinoa, amaranth, buckwheat and chia seeds contain all 9 essential amino acids and are therefore classified as complete proteins.

PULSES
Dried beans, peas and lentils are a major source of protein in a vegetable-based diet as they can be eaten in place of animal protein sources and in lower-protein carbs such as rice and potatoes. They are also rich in various vitamins and minerals as well as fibre and plant chemicals.

NUTS AND SEEDS
Though we tend to eat nuts and seeds in smaller quantity, they are a valuable protein source as well as containing important unsaturated fats and a variety of vitamins and minerals, fibre and plant chemicals.

GRAINS AND PSEUDO GRAINS
Rolled oats and whole wheat are popular and traditionally thought of as carb foods but are surprisingly high in protein. Other grains, such as spelt, wild rice, quinoa (not actually a grain but a seed) and amaranth contain very useful amounts of protein.

VEGETABLES
All plant foods contain at least some protein, and several vegetables supply good amounts, including leafy greens such as spinach, cabbage and broccoli, fresh peas and beans.

EGGS AND DAIRY-BASED PROTEINS

Milk, cheese and yogurt are an important part of a protein-rich diet for many vegetarians, and they are also a great source of calcium, while eggs contain a range of vitamins and minerals.

EGGS
Several research studies on eggs show that a breakfast or meal containing eggs can help reduce hunger throughout the day and limit calorie intake. They are a good source of B vitamins as well as iron, zinc and selenium.

Egg whites are cholesterol free, low-calorie and 85% protein. An average egg contains only a third of its fat as saturates while over a third are healthy monounsaturates.

If you buy organic eggs from hens allowed unlimited access to organic pastures and woodland they will naturally have a higher content of omega-3 fats, the healthy unsaturated group also found (in another form) in oily fish, a lower saturates level and more vitamin E.

MILK AND YOGURT
Milk and yogurt can make a useful contribution to your daily protein intake. Not all milk and yogurt is high in saturated fat, as is often thought. For example, full fat Greek yogurt contains a higher level of protein than other types of yogurt and its saturated fat content is relatively low.

Milk and yogurt are good sources of calcium for healthy bones as well as B vitamins. Full-fat milk is also a good source of vitamin A – low-fat versions are not, as the vitamin is found only in the fat.

Sheep and goat's milk and yogurt are becoming more popular and more available.

CHEESE
Cheese is often thought of as one of the best sources of protein but some varieties have a much higher content than others.

Hard cheeses, such as Cheddar, Parmesan and Gruyère are some of the best, while creamy and soft cheeses are often low in protein – the exceptions being soft goat's cheese, ricotta and quark/fromage frais.

Hard cheeses are a good source of calcium and B vitamins while full-fat cheeses are a good source of vitamin A.

Organic milk, yogurt and cheese tend to contain a better ratio of healthy unsaturated fats to saturated fats.

Meals and snacks containing cheese help to increase satiety and keep hunger at bay for longer.

MEAT AND FISH PROTEINS

Red and white meats, poultry and fish have been recommended for decades as the best source of top quality 'complete protein'. But in recent years there has been much conflicting evidence and advice about how much of them we should eat.

WHAT DOES TOP QUALITY PROTEIN MEAN?

Top quality protein means a protein source that contains all the essential amino acids in good proportions, and which are easily absorbed by the digestive system. Animal sources of protein such as lean meat and fish are excellent sources of top quality complete proteins which are also well absorbed by most people.

DO WE NEED MEAT AND FISH?

No – vegetarian and vegan diets can, with care, provide the full range of nutrients. However, vegetables and meat/fish contain different nutrients needed for health (e.g. red meat is high in easily-absorbed iron and zinc while pulses contain less; pulses are rich in fibre while meats contain none; oily fish is a great source of omega-3 fat while vegetables contain little), so a diet which combines both could be an easy way to ensure all the nutrients you need.

But we shouldn't eat too much red meat (beef, lamb, pork, veal, venison or goat). Recent advice from health departments across the world is that we should limit our intake to no more than 70g a day or 500g a week, because high intake may be linked with bowel cancer.

The best idea is to use it as a small component of a meal rather than 'the main event'. Because gram for gram, meat is higher in protein than most other protein sources, you can eat less and still meet your protein needs.

Chicken (and other birds) don't fall under official advice on limitation. Choose lean chicken and avoid the fatty skin. Turkey breast is a very low-fat and high protein choice.

CAN WE EAT FISH FREELY?

Rather than limiting our intake of fish, UK Department of Health advice is that we should try to eat more – most of us can have as much white fish as we like and at least one 140g portion of omega-3 rich oily fish such as salmon or mackerel a week but no more than four. All fish and seafoods are a complete protein source and contain a range of vitamins and minerals.

PROTEIN FOR YOUR HEALTH

Most people realise that protein helps build muscle and keeps us strong, but it has a wide range of other benefits within your body and for your health. Protein is essential for building, maintaining and repairing cells and for the actual structure of cells. Each of the nine essential amino acids has its own role to play in keeping the body and mind healthy.

THE NINE ESSENTIAL AMINO ACIDS

ISOLEUCINE: Helps produce haemoglobin for healthy blood; aids muscle recovery after exercise. It is found in soya, beef, pork, tuna.

LEUCINE: Promotes growth and healing. It is found in soya, beef, pork, tuna.

LYSINE: For a healthy nervous system and hormonal balance. It is found in pork, chicken, cod, sardines.

METHIONINE: Important for fat metabolism, muscle and cartilage maintenance; anti-inflammatory. It is found in tuna, salmon, hard cheese, nuts.

PHENYLALANINE: Can help prevent depression and maintain memory; controls satiety. It is found in beef, fish, shellfish, cheese, milk, nuts, soya.

THREONINE: Boosts the immune system, helps build collagen for good skin. It is found in turkey, eggs, soya.

TRYPTOPHAN: Helps promote good sleep, helps prevent migraines and depression. It is found in turkey, chicken, shellfish, milk, yogurt, nuts, seeds, pulses.

VALINE: Essential for muscle development. It is found in turkey, chicken, dairy produce, soya, lentils, black beans.

HISTIDINE: For growth and development, production of blood cells and circulation. It is found in beef, Parmesan, soya, poultry, oily fish, seeds.

EATING PROTEIN THROUGHOUT THE DAY

It's not hard to ensure that you get enough protein every day. If you get a varied diet, including a range of different protein sources and adding in plenty of different-coloured vegetables, salad items and fruits at each meal you will ensure you get the complete range of amino acids as well as all the vitamins, minerals, fats, fibre and carbs you need for good health. Our recipes offer an exciting selection of meals and snacks for all occasions.

START THE DAY WITH PROTEIN

A high-protein breakfast is the ideal way to start the day. It will keep you feeling full until lunchtime, help your brain feel alert, and is a good chance to pack in the other nutrients that high protein foods offer.

Many protein foods are quick and easy to cook – eggs really are a perfect breakfast food and if you add in fruits or vegetables high in vitamin C this will help their minerals to be better absorbed.

PACK HIGH-PROTEIN PORTABLE SNACKS

If you lead an active life and are always busy or dashing about, having one or two high-protein snacks in your bag or case is an easy way to ensure you don't succumb to bought snacks high in white carbs, sugar, fat and salt.

Try a bag of unsalted nuts, or take a mix of nuts and seeds such as almonds, cashews, pumpkin seeds and sunflower seeds. Or try a hard-boiled egg or a seed cracker topped with peanut butter.

IDEAS FOR SNACKING AFTER SPORT

If you've been busy working out, running or on the playing field, it's a good idea to have a high-protein snack, with a small amount of carbohydrate added for instant energy replacement.

Make sure your sports bag contains such a snack – ideas include a healthy smoothie made with milled flaxseed, almond butter, milk and banana; some cacao nibs mixed with walnuts; 25 g/1 oz Gruyère cheese with 1 small apple; roasted cooked chickpeas sprinkled with paprika.

EASY INGREDIENT SWAPS FOR EVERYDAY MEALS

~ Replace potatoes with mashed or puréed cannellini or butter beans.
~ Replace rice with quinoa.
~ Choose seed crackers instead of bread.
~ Choose buckwheat noodles instead of pasta.
~ Swap croûtons on your salad for lightly toasted nuts and seeds.
~ Making a wrap – choose lettuce leaves instead of the bread.

BREAKFASTS

Pea and kale frittatas	20
Savoury oatmeal with hot smoked salmon and avocado	22
Crushed edamame and avocado toasts	24
Orange and banana pancakes	26
Roasted almond gingersnap butter	28
Nutty granola sundaes with yogurt and mango	30
Quinoa and cashew nut porridge	32
Fruity puffed quinoa with pumpkin seeds	34
Spinach and nutmeg baked eggs	36
Three herb and ricotta omelette	38
Berry power smoothie	40
Linseed and chia chocolate smoothie	42

PEA AND KALE FRITTATAS

These mini frittatas are really simple to make and packed with protein from all the eggs. Filling them with a yummy combination of peas and kale makes them even more nutritious.

MAKES: 12 FRITTATAS
PREP: 10 MINS, PLUS COOLING   COOK: 25–30 MINS

10 g/¼ oz butter, for greasing
1 tbsp olive oil
4 spring onions, trimmed and chopped
100 g/3½ oz frozen peas, thawed
50 g/1¾ oz kale, shredded
6 eggs
100 ml/3½ fl oz milk
100 g/3½ oz feta cheese, crumbled
salt and pepper (optional)

1. Preheat the oven to 180°C/350°F/Gas Mark 4. Grease a 12-hole muffin tin and set aside.

2. Heat the olive oil in a frying pan and cook the spring onions over a medium heat for 3–4 minutes, until beginning to soften.

3. Add the peas and kale to the pan and cook for a further 2–3 minutes.

4. Beat the eggs and milk together in a bowl and season to taste with salt and pepper, if using.

5. Divide the pea and kale mixture between the holes in your prepared tin and pour some eggy milk over each one.

6. Sprinkle the feta cheese over the top of each frittata and bake in the preheated oven for 18–20 minutes, until golden and set.

7. Allow the frittatas to cool for a few minutes, then remove from the tin with a spatula. Eat them warm or cold.

WHY NOT TRY?
Try out different fillings – make your frittatas with bacon and asparagus, or tomato and basil.

PER FRITTATA: 89 KCALS | 6.3G FAT | 2.8G SAT FAT | 2.8G CARBS | 1.5G SUGARS | 0.7G FIBRE | 5.3G PROTEIN | 0.3G SALT

SAVOURY OATMEAL WITH HOT SMOKED SALMON AND AVOCADO

You may think porridge is just a sweet breakfast, but oats taste great with savoury flavours and provide sustained energy through the morning. Adding salmon gives a protein and omega-3 boost.

SERVES: 4
PREP: 10 MINS   COOK: 12–15 MINS

150 g/5½ oz rolled oats
350 ml/12 fl oz milk
600 ml/1 pint water
4 eggs
4 tsp creamed horseradish
200 g/7 oz hot smoked salmon, flaked
2 avocados, stoned, peeled and sliced
freshly milled black pepper (optional)
2 tbsp pumpkin seeds, toasted, to garnish

1. Place the oats in a saucepan with the milk and water. Bring to the boil and then simmer for 4–5 minutes, until thick and creamy.

2. Meanwhile, poach the eggs in a pan of simmering water for 4–5 minutes.

3. Stir the creamed horseradish and half the smoked salmon into the porridge.

4. Divide the porridge between four warmed bowls and top each one with slices of avocado, a poached egg and the remaining salmon.

5. Serve the porridge sprinkled with toasted pumpkin seeds and seasoned to taste with pepper, if using.

SOMETHING DIFFERENT
Sautéed mushrooms topped with a fried egg and a sprinkling of chives make a delicious variation.

PER SERVING: 547 KCALS | 32.8G FAT | 7.1G SAT FAT | 37.9G CARBS | 6G SUGARS | 9.1G FIBRE | 27.7G PROTEIN | 1.3G SALT

CRUSHED EDAMAME AND AVOCADO TOASTS

Edamame beans are rich in protein and avocado is full of omega-3 fats. Sprinkled with toasted sunflower seeds and slathered over thick slices of sourdough, this is a perfect, tasty breakfast.

SERVES: 4
PREP: 10 MINS   COOK: 8–10 MINS

125 g/4½ oz frozen edamame beans, thawed
3 tbsp sunflower seeds
8 slices sourdough bread
2 tbsp tahini paste
1 tbsp lime juice
2 avocados, stoned, peeled and chopped
½ small red onion, thinly sliced
salt and pepper (optional)
2 tbsp avocado oil, to serve

1. Place the edamame beans in a microwavable container and microwave for 4½ minutes. Leave to cool for a few minutes before removing the beans.

2. Toast the sunflower seeds in a dry pan over medium heat for 2–3 minutes.

3. Toast the sourdough on both sides.

4. Place the edamame beans in a bowl with the tahini, lime juice and avocado, and roughly crush with a fork.

5. Spoon the edamame mixture onto the toasts, then sprinkle with the toasted seeds and slices of onion. Season to taste with salt and pepper, if using.

6. Drizzle with avocado oil to serve.

COOK'S TIP
Other protein-rich toast toppers include poached eggs, smoked salmon, hummus and peppered steak.

PER SERVING: 478 KCALS | 28.9G FAT | 3.8G SAT FAT | 43.4G CARBS | 4.4G SUGARS | 9.2G FIBRE | 14.7G PROTEIN | 0.9G SALT

ORANGE AND BANANA PANCAKES

Teff flour is milled from a fine grain grown mainly in Ethiopia, known for its health-boosting and gluten-free properties. It has a subtle nutty flavour and complements pancakes beautifully.

SERVES: 4

PREP: 5–10 MINS   COOK: 25 MINS

125 g/4½ oz teff flour
½ tsp ground cinnamon
1 tsp baking powder
1 egg
175 ml/6 fl oz milk
30 g/1 oz unsalted butter, melted
1 banana, peeled and diced
1 tbsp melted coconut oil

TO SERVE
2 oranges, peeled and segmented
1 tbsp sesame seeds, toasted
maple syrup (optional)

1. Mix the flour, cinnamon and baking powder together in a large bowl.

2. Whisk the egg and milk together in a separate bowl, then whisk into the flour mixture until smooth – the batter should be the consistency of thick, double cream. Add a little more milk if needed.

3. Stir the melted butter and banana into the pancake batter.

4. Heat the coconut oil in a frying pan over a medium heat, then spoon in tablespoons of the batter. Cook for 3–4 minutes, until the pancakes are golden underneath, then flip over and cook for a further 2–3 minutes.

5. Repeat with the remaining batter until you have 12 pancakes.

6. Serve the pancakes topped with the orange segments, a sprinkling of toasted sesame seeds and a drizzle of maple syrup, if using.

WHY NOT TRY?
These pancakes can be served with other fresh fruits, honey or a dollop of natural yogurt.

PER SERVING: 315 KCALS | 14.1G FAT | 8.2G SAT FAT | 40.2G CARBS | 12.5G SUGARS | 5.1G FIBRE | 9G PROTEIN | 0.4G SALT

ROASTED ALMOND GINGERSNAP BUTTER

Lightly sweetened with treacle and brown sugar, and spiced with both fresh and ground ginger, this healthy nut butter tastes just like gingersnap biscuits. Try it spread on crisp apples as a light snack or have it on toast with sliced pears.

MAKES: 350 G/12 OZ
PREP: 10 MINS   COOK: NONE

285 g/10¼ oz roasted almonds
2 tbsp soft light brown sugar
2 tbsp black treacle
1½ tsp grated fresh ginger
½ tsp ground ginger
¼ tsp salt
2–3 tbsp grapeseed oil
1 apple, sliced, to serve (optional)

1. Put the almonds into a food processor and process for 5–10 minutes, until smooth.

2. Add the sugar, treacle, fresh ginger, ground ginger, and salt and process until well combined. With the processor running, add the oil, a little at a time, until you achieve the desired consistency.

3. Serve immediately on a sliced apple, if liked, or refrigerate until ready to use. Almond butter can be stored in the refrigerator for several weeks.

COOK'S TIP
It can take a while for almonds to release their oils so that your almond butter has the consistency you're after. Don't give up. Keep processing (giving your food processor a break now and then if it begins to overheat) until you get a smooth, creamy paste, which could take as long as 10 minutes or more.

PER 350 G/12 OZ: 2204 KCALS | 182.3G FAT | 14.8G SAT FAT | 110.5G CARBS | 63G SUGARS | 31.2G FIBRE | 60.5G PROTEIN | 1.5G SALT

NUTTY GRANOLA SUNDAES WITH YOGURT AND MANGO

Making your own granola is so easy, and means you can include the ingredients you like and take out the ones you don't! It is also cheaper than shop-bought granola and tastes delicious.

SERVES: 6
PREP: 10–15 MINS   COOK: 35–40 MINS

100 g/3¹⁄₂ oz whole almonds, roughly chopped
75 g/2³⁄₄ oz pecan nuts, roughly chopped
50 g/1³⁄₄ oz cashew nuts, roughly chopped
50 g/1³⁄₄ oz sunflower seeds
100 g/3¹⁄₂ oz pumpkin seeds
2 tbsp sesame seeds
125 g/4¹⁄₂ oz rolled oats
3 tbsp coconut oil
3 tbsp maple syrup
2 tsp ground cinnamon
100 g/3¹⁄₂ oz dried cranberries
8 tbsp Greek-style yogurt
1 mango, stoned, peeled and chopped

1. Preheat the oven to 180°C/350°F/Gas Mark 4.

2. Place the nuts in a large bowl with the seeds and oats, and mix well.

3. In a small pan, combine the coconut oil with the maple syrup and cinnamon over a medium heat. When the coconut oil has melted, remove from the heat and stir into the nut mixture, mixing well.

4. Spread the mixture over a baking sheet and bake in the preheated oven for 30–35 minutes, shaking and stirring from time to time, until golden.

5. Allow the granola to cool before stirring in the cranberries.

6. Divide the granola between six bowls and serve layered with yogurt and chopped mango.

GO FOR A VARIETY
The choice of nuts and seeds is up to you, but a wide variety is always best to gain the most nutrients available.

PER SERVING: 646 KCALS | 44.4G FAT | 10.9G SAT FAT | 52.6G CARBS | 25.9G SUGARS | 9.3G FIBRE | 19G PROTEIN | TRACE SALT

QUINOA AND CASHEW NUT PORRIDGE

Creamy and delicious porridge doesn't have to be made with oats!
Quinoa provides much more protein and doesn't contain any wheat.
Cashew nuts also add essential minerals including magnesium and potassium.

SERVES: 4
PREP: 5–10 MINS   COOK: 12–15 MINS

175 g/6 oz quinoa
30 g/1 oz cashew nuts, roughly chopped
1 litre/1³/4 pints almond milk
1 vanilla pod, split and seeds removed
1 apple, grated
1 tsp ground cinnamon
1 tbsp maple syrup
2 tbsp chia seeds

TO SERVE
100 g/3¹/2 oz raspberries
50 g/1³/4 oz blueberries
2 tbsp pomegranate seeds

1. Place the quinoa in a pan with the nuts, milk, vanilla seeds, apple, cinnamon and maple syrup. Bring to the boil, then simmer for 10–12 minutes.

2. Stir the chia seeds into the pan and stir well.

3. Spoon the porridge into four bowls and serve topped with the raspberries, blueberries and pomegranate seeds.

MIX IT UP
Serve this porridge with the fruit and nuts of your choice. Try to use fruits that are in season, such as berries in the summer, and apples and pears through the winter months.

PER SERVING: 332 KCALS | 11G FAT | 1.1G SAT FAT | 49.9G CARBS | 10.7G SUGARS | 9G FIBRE | 13.4G PROTEIN | 0.4G SALT

FRUITY PUFFED QUINOA WITH PUMPKIN SEEDS

Quinoa puffs are a healthy alternative to regular breakfast cereal. Here, apple juice is used to moisten the puffs instead of the more commonly used milk. It makes a particularly refreshing start to the day!

SERVES: 1
PREP: 10 MINS   COOK: NONE

25 g/1 oz puffed quinoa
125 ml/4 fl oz apple juice
1 small banana, thinly sliced
½ crisp, red-skinned apple, sliced into thin segments
2 tsp pumpkin seeds
1 tbsp honey, for drizzling
2 tbsp Greek-style yogurt, to serve

1. Put the puffed quinoa into a serving bowl. Stir in the apple juice, making sure the puffs are submerged. Leave to stand for a few minutes.

2. Arrange the banana slices and apple segments on top of the quinoa.

3. Scatter over the pumpkin seeds and drizzle with a little honey. Serve immediately with yogurt.

WHY NOT TRY?
For a delicious variation, try using freshly squeezed orange juice instead of the apple juice. You could also replace the apples with pears.

PER SERVING: 393 KCALS | 5.1G FAT | 1.7G SAT FAT | 84.6G CARBS | 50.5G SUGARS | 5.7G FIBRE | 7G PROTEIN | TRACE SALT

SPINACH AND NUTMEG BAKED EGGS

Nutrient-rich fresh spinach adds delicious flavour and colour to this popular egg dish, lightly seasoned with ground nutmeg. Serve with standard or gluten-free bread for a wholesome breakfast or brunch.

SERVES: 4
PREP: 20 MINS   COOK: 20–30 MINS

1 tbsp olive oil, for brushing
1 tbsp olive oil, for frying
4 shallots, finely chopped
3 garlic cloves, sliced
100 g/3½ oz baby spinach
8 eggs
½ tsp ground nutmeg
salt and pepper (optional)

1. Preheat the oven to 180°C/350°F/Gas Mark 4. Lightly brush the insides of four 200 ml/7 fl oz ramekins with olive oil.

2. Heat the olive oil in a frying pan. Once hot, add the shallots and garlic and fry over a medium heat for 3–4 minutes, or until soft. Add the baby spinach and stir for 2–3 minutes, or until just wilted. Season with salt and pepper, if using.

3. Spoon the spinach mixture into the bottom of the prepared ramekins and crack two eggs into each. Sprinkle over the nutmeg and place the ramekins in a roasting tin. Fill the roasting tin with boiling water until the water reaches halfway up the ramekins – this creates a steamy environment for the eggs so there is no chance of them drying out.

4. Carefully transfer the roasting tin to the preheated oven for 15–20 minutes. Leave the ramekins to cool slightly then serve immediately.

SUPER SPINACH
Researchers have found many flavonoid compounds in spinach act as antioxidants and fight against stomach, skin, breast, prostate and other cancers.

PER SERVING: 235 KCALS | 16.5G FAT | 4.2G SAT FAT | 7.5G CARBS | 1.6G SUGARS | 1.1G FIBRE | 14.2G PROTEIN | 0.4G SALT

THREE HERB AND RICOTTA OMELETTE

Vibrant green mixed garden herbs add lots of lovely natural flavour and colour to this appetizing omelette. Served with fresh bread to accompany, it's just the ticket for a satisfying breakfast for two.

SERVES: 2
PREP: 15 MINS   COOK: 8 MINS

4 large eggs
2 tbsp finely snipped fresh chives
2 tbsp finely chopped fresh basil
2 tbsp finely chopped fresh parsley
100 g/3½ oz ricotta cheese, crumbled
2 tbsp olive oil
salt and pepper (optional)

1. Crack the eggs into a small mixing bowl and lightly beat with a fork. Stir the herbs and ricotta into the bowl and season with salt and pepper, if using.

2. Heat the olive oil in a non-stick frying pan over a high heat until hot. Pour in the egg mixture and, using a spatula, draw the outside edges (which will cook more quickly) towards the gooey centre. Allow any liquid mixture to move into the gaps. Continue with this action for about 4–5 minutes. The omelette will continue to cook once the pan is removed from the heat.

3. Cut the omelette in half and divide between two plates. Serve immediately.

EXCELLENT EGGS
Eggs contain high-quality protein, the macronutrient that best satisfies hunger. They also contain essential vitamins, including vitamin A, needed for healthy skin and good vision.

PER SERVING: 390 KCALS | 32G FAT | 10G SAT FAT | 2.8G CARBS | 0.7G SUGARS | 0.2G FIBRE | 21.7G PROTEIN | 0.6G SALT

BERRY POWER SMOOTHIE

*Breakfast is arguably the most important meal of the day,
and this shake includes lots of vital nutrients. It's quick to make,
tasty and filling, but won't leave you feeling heavy.*

SERVES: 1
PREP: 15 MINS   COOK: NONE

20 g/³/₄ oz pumpkin seeds
20 g/³/₄ oz flaxseeds
20 g/³/₄ oz flaked almonds
115 g/4 oz raspberries
115 g/4 oz blueberries
225 g/8 oz vanilla soya yogurt
125 ml/4 fl oz chilled water

1. Put the pumpkin seeds, flaxseeds and almonds in a blender and blend until finely ground.

2. Add the raspberries, blueberries, yogurt and chilled water and blend until smooth.

3. Pour into a glass and serve.

POWERFUL PUMPKIN SEEDS
These little seeds are really nutritious and, even in small servings they provide a significant amount of minerals, especially zinc and iron.

PER SERVING: 641 KCALS | 33.8G FAT | 3.7G SAT FAT | 72.7G CARBS | 41.8G SUGARS | 19.9G FIBRE | 22.1G PROTEIN | 0.1G SALT

LINSEED AND CHIA CHOCOLATE SMOOTHIE

A chocolate smoothie sounds indulgent but this recipe includes nutritious ingredients, such as linseeds for added fibre, chia seeds for omega-3 fats and a raw egg for that extra boost of protein.

SERVES: 2
PREP: 5 MINS   COOK: NONE

300 ml/10 fl oz pint milk
1 banana, peeled and chopped
2 tsp ground linseeds
1 tsp ground chia seeds
3 tsp cacao powder
1 egg

1. Place all the ingredients in a blender and blend until smooth.

2. Pour the smoothie into two glasses and serve.

DID YOU KNOW?
While eggs are a rich source of protein, infants, the elderly, pregnant women, convalescents and anyone suffering from an illness should avoid eating raw eggs.

PER SERVING: 210 KCALS | 9.6G FAT | 4G SAT FAT | 24G CARBS | 14.9G SUGARS | 4G FIBRE | 9.8G PROTEIN | 0.2G SALT

LUNCHES AND SNACKS

SALMON AND SOYA BEAN SALAD

Salmon is a real superfood – not only delicious, but rich in protein and omega-3 fats, which are hugely important for physical and mental health.

SERVES: 4
PREP: 15 MINS   COOK: 6–8 MINS

400 g/14 oz salmon fillets
200 g/7 oz frozen soya beans, thawed
200 g/7 oz frozen peas, thawed
100 g/3½ oz roasted red pepper, cut into strips
40 g/1½ oz fresh rocket
15 g/½ oz fresh dill, chopped
pepper (optional)

DRESSING
3 tbsp olive oil
1½ tbsp lemon juice
1 tsp wholegrain mustard
1 tsp honey

1. For the dressing, whisk the olive oil, lemon juice, mustard and honey together in a small bowl. Set aside.

2. Grill the salmon fillets under a medium heat for 3–4 minutes on each side, until the fish is opaque and flaky when separated with a fork. Break into large flakes.

3. Meanwhile bring a large saucepan of water to the boil and tip the soya beans and peas into the water. Cook for 3–4 minutes, until just tender. Drain and run under cold water to refresh.

4. Place the salmon flakes, beans, peas, pepper strips, rocket and dill in a large bowl. Pour over the dressing and season to taste with pepper, if using. Toss well to combine. Divide between four bowls and serve.

ALSO TRY...
Other beans, such as canned cannellini beans or butter beans, work perfectly in this recipe.

PER SERVING: 446 KCALS | 30.3G FAT | 5.2G SAT FAT | 13G CARBS | 5.8G SUGARS | 5.1G FIBRE | 29.9G PROTEIN | 0.3G SALT

HARISSA CHICKEN SALAD

Capture the flavours and colours of Morocco with this spicy brown rice salad flecked with jewel-like diced dried apricots and glistening raisins, and tossed with health-boosting green kale.

SERVES: 4
PREP: 10–15 MINS   COOK: 30–35 MINS

250 g/9 oz easy–cook brown rice
2 tsp tomato purée
500 g/1 lb 2 oz skinless chicken breast fillets
85 g/3 oz ready–to–eat dried apricots, diced
55 g/2 oz raisins
55 g/2 oz pickled lemons, drained and finely chopped
1 small red onion, finely chopped
85 g/3 oz kale, shredded
3 tbsp pine nuts, toasted

DRESSING
2 tsp harissa
4 tbsp olive oil
juice of 1 lemon
salt and pepper (optional)

1. Put the rice in a saucepan of boiling water. Bring back to the boil, then simmer for 25–30 minutes, or until tender. Drain, then transfer to a salad bowl.

2. Meanwhile, to make the dressing, put the harissa, oil and lemon juice in a jam jar, season to taste with salt and pepper, if using, screw on the lid and shake well.

3. Spoon 2 tablespoons of the dressing into a bowl and mix in the tomato purée. Preheat the grill to high and line the grill pan with foil. Put the chicken on the foil in a single layer. Brush some of the tomato dressing over the chicken, then grill for 15–18 minutes, or until golden and cooked through, turning the meat and brushing it with the remaining tomato dressing halfway through cooking. Cut through the middle of a breast to check that the meat is no longer pink and any juices run clear and are piping hot. Cover and leave to cool.

4. Drizzle the remaining dressing over the rice in the salad bowl. Add the dried apricots, raisins, pickled lemons and onion, then toss gently together and leave to cool.

5. Add the kale and pine nuts to the salad and stir well. Thinly slice the chicken, arrange it over the salad and serve.

HEALTH-GIVING RICE
Rice is an important source of protein and energy. Easy-cook brown rice has a little of the bran removed and is parboiled before milling, speeding up cooking but retaining far more of the vital nutrients and fibre than white rice. Homeopaths believe that rice can help treat digestive disorders, from indigestion to diverticulitis.

PER SERVING: 668 KCALS | 24G FAT | 3.1G SAT FAT | 78.8G CARBS | 22.1G SUGARS | 6.4G FIBRE | 36.3G PROTEIN | 0.9G SALT

POKE BOWL

A poke bowl is a staple Hawaiian dish that normally contains raw fish and lots of vibrant ingredients, both hot and cold. This recipe includes tuna for protein and wakame for magnesium, iodine and calcium.

SERVES: 4

PREP: 15 MINS, PLUS SOAKING   COOK: 25 MINS

200 g/7 oz brown rice
15 g/½ oz wakame, soaked in lukewarm water for 10–15 minutes and roughly chopped
2 tbsp soy sauce
2 tbsp rice wine vinegar
225 g/8 oz good-quality raw tuna, sliced
1 avocado, stoned, peeled and sliced
8 cherry tomatoes, halved
4 spring onions, thinly sliced
½ tsp chilli flakes
2 tbsp olive oil
1 tbsp black sesame seeds

1. Cook the rice according to the packet instructions.

2. Place the cooked rice in a bowl and stir in half the soaked wakame, half the soy sauce and the rice wine vinegar. Divide between four bowls and top with the tuna, avocado, tomatoes and spring onions.

3. Mix the remaining soy sauce and wakame with the chilli flakes, olive oil and sesame seeds in a small bowl. Sprinkle over the poke bowls to serve.

A FLASH IN THE PAN
If you don't want to eat your fish raw, flash-fry it quickly in a pan before adding to your dish.

PER SERVING: 399 KCALS | 15.4G FAT | 2.2G SAT FAT | 45.5G CARBS | 2.4G SUGARS | 5.3G FIBRE | 20.4G PROTEIN | 1.3G SALT

CHICKEN NOODLE PROTEIN SOUP

This classic chicken soup is an easy, nutritious lunch and can be made in advance. It's full of health benefits – red chillies lower cholesterol and soba noodles are made from gluten-free buckwheat flour.

SERVES: 4
PREP: 20 MINS   COOK: 20 MINS

1 litre/1³/4 pints chicken stock
1 tbsp soy sauce
1 garlic clove, crushed
1 red chilli, deseeded and finely chopped
3–cm/1¹/4–inch piece fresh root ginger, peeled and grated
500 g/1 lb 2 oz skinless, boneless chicken breasts
4 eggs
400 g/14 oz soba noodles
100 g/3¹/2 oz sweetcorn
4 pak choi, cut lengthways into quarters
1 tbsp sesame oil, for drizzling

1. Place the stock, soy sauce, garlic, chilli and ginger in a saucepan and bring to the boil. Add the chicken and simmer for 10–12 minutes, until the chicken is tender and the juices run clear when a skewer is inserted into the thickest part of the meat. Remove the chicken with a slotted spoon.

2. Meanwhile, boil the eggs for 4–5 minutes in a pan of boiling water. Refresh under cold water. Drain and peel the eggs.

3. Return the stock to the heat, bring to a simmer and add the noodles. Cook for 2 minutes, or according to the packet instructions. Add the sweetcorn and pak choi, and simmer for another 2 minutes.

4. Shred or thickly slice the chicken and return to the pan with the stock and noodles to heat through for 1 minute.

5. Serve the soup in four warmed bowls with halved soft-boiled eggs on top and drizzled with the sesame oil.

WHY NOT TRY?
You can make this soup with a mixture of fish stock, white fish and prawns if you don't want chicken.

PER SERVING: 677 KCALS | 14.3G FAT | 3.3G SAT FAT | 80.7G CARBS | 12.2G SUGARS | 5G FIBRE | 52.7G PROTEIN | 3G SALT

LENTIL AND CHICKPEA SOUP

Mixing vegetable proteins, such as rice and lentils, ensures an intake of essential amino acids. This soup has a variety of vegetables, plus lots of tantalizing spices for nutrition and flavour.

SERVES: 4
PREP: 10 MINS   COOK: 25 MINS

150 g/5½ oz brown rice
2 tsp cumin seeds
¼ tsp chilli flakes
1½ tbsp melted coconut oil, for frying
1 red onion, peeled and chopped
140 g/5 oz red split lentils
850 ml/1½ pints vegetable stock
1 x 400 g/14 oz can chopped tomatoes
200 g/7 oz canned chickpeas, drained and rinsed
4 spring onions, trimmed and sliced
200 g/7 oz canned Puy lentils, drained and rinsed
salt and pepper (optional)
4 tbsp Greek-style yogurt, to serve
15 g/½ oz fresh coriander leaves, to serve

1. Cook the rice according to the packet instructions.

2. Meanwhile, fry the cumin seeds and chilli flakes in a dry saucepan over a medium heat for 1 minute before adding 1 tablespoon of the coconut oil.

3. Add the red onion to the saucepan and cook for 3–4 minutes. Stir in the lentils, stock, tomatoes and half the chickpeas, and bring to the boil. Simmer for 15 minutes, until the lentils have softened.

4. Meanwhile, heat the remaining oil in a separate pan and sauté the spring onions over a medium heat for 3–4 minutes before stirring in the Puy lentils. Cook for 1–2 minutes to heat through.

5. Using a hand blender, blend the soup in the saucepan until smooth. Season to taste with salt and pepper, if using.

6. Pour the soup into four warmed bowls and add a spoonful of rice, the remaining chickpeas, the spring onions and Puy lentils to each one. Serve topped with a dollop of yogurt and a sprinkling of coriander.

LOVELY LENTILS
Lentils are a rich source of fibre, which helps protect against cancer and cardiovascular disease.

PER SERVING: 457 KCALS | 11G FAT | 6.3G SAT FAT | 71.4G CARBS | 7.4G SUGARS | 10.3G FIBRE | 19.7G PROTEIN | 2G SALT

COURGETTE AND BEAN TACOS

*Tacos and homemade guacamole can be a scrumptious snack
or light lunch. This recipe includes a salad made with cannellini
beans for protein, plus crunchy celery, carrot and courgette for extra fibre.*

SERVES: 4

PREP: 12 MINS, PLUS COOLING   COOK: 30 MINS

TACO SHELLS
2 courgettes, grated
120 g/4¼ oz freshly grated Parmesan cheese
100 g/3½ oz fresh breadcrumbs
2 eggs, beaten
salt and pepper (optional)

GUACAMOLE
1 red chilli, deseeded and finely diced
juice of ½ lime
2 ripe avocados, stoned and peeled

TACO FILLING
2 celery stalks, thinly sliced
1 courgette, diced
1 carrot, peeled and grated
1 small red onion, peeled and diced
2 x 400 g/14 oz cans cannellini beans, drained and rinsed
8 cherry tomatoes, quartered
2 tbsp chopped fresh coriander
2 tbsp extra virgin olive oil

TO SERVE
35 g /1¼ oz fresh watercress
4 tbsp natural yogurt
2 tbsp pumpkin seeds, toasted

1. Preheat the oven to 200°C/400°F/Gas Mark 6. Line two baking sheets with non-stick baking paper and set aside.

2. To make the taco shells, wrap the grated courgettes in kitchen paper and squeeze as much moisture from them as possible. Mix the courgettes, cheese, breadcrumbs and eggs together in a bowl. Season to taste with salt and pepper, if using.

3. Spread the mixture into 8 circles on the prepared baking sheets. Bake in the preheated oven for 20 minutes.

4. Turn the taco shells over and bake for a further 10 minutes, then remove from the baking sheets and lay over a rolling pin to help them curl. Leave to cool.

5. Meanwhile, make the guacamole. Place the chilli, lime juice and avocados in a small bowl and mash together until smooth. Set aside.

6. To make the taco filling, mix the celery, courgette, carrot, onion, beans, tomatoes, coriander and olive oil together in a bowl.

7. Divide the watercress between the cooled taco shells, then spoon the bean mix into each one.

8. Top each taco with a dollop of guacamole and yogurt, and sprinkle with toasted pumpkin seeds to serve.

HEALTHY COURGETTES
Courgettes provide immune-system-boosting vitamin C, and significant levels of potassium, which help control blood pressure.

PER SERVING: 621 KCALS | 33G FAT | 9.3G SAT FAT | 50.3G CARBS | 10.6G SUGARS | 17.4G FIBRE | 31.2G PROTEIN | 1.6G SALT

SPICY PARSNIP YOGURT WITH FLATBREADS

Thick yogurt is transformed into a savoury dip by stirring in a parsnip purée and topping with spices and herbs. The flatbreads are made from ground chickpeas for increased protein and fibre.

SERVES: 4
PREP: 15 MINS, PLUS STANDING   COOK: 40–50 MINS

1 large parsnip, peeled and chopped
400 g /14 oz Greek-style yogurt
3 tsp harrisa paste
2 tbsp canned chickpeas, rinsed
1 tbsp snipped fresh chives
2 large egg whites

FLATBREADS

250 g/9 oz gram flour
50 g/1¾ oz buckwheat flour
1 tsp baking powder
1 tsp cumin seeds
400 ml/14 fl oz water
1 tbsp olive oil, for frying
salt and pepper (optional)

1. To make the flatbreads, place the flours, baking powder and cumin in a large bowl. Season to taste with salt and pepper, if using. Whisk in the water, until smooth. Set aside for 90 minutes so the mixture can soak up the water.

2. Meanwhile, cook the parsnip in a pan of boiling water for 12–15 minutes, until soft. Drain and blend to a purée in a small blender.

3. Mix the yogurt and harissa paste in a bowl, leaving swirls of both (do not combine completely). Sprinkle with the chickpeas and chives.

4. When the flatbread batter is ready, whisk the egg whites in a small bowl until they are stiff. Fold them into the flatbread batter.

5. Heat the olive oil in a large frying pan and pour in a quarter of the batter. Cook for 3–4 minutes over a medium heat, until the top starts to bubble and the bottom is golden. Flip over and cook for a further 3–4 minutes, until golden on both sides. Remove from the pan and repeat with the remaining batter.

6. Serve the flatbreads with the spicy parsnip yogurt.

MAKE IT SWEET
The flatbread can also be turned into a sweet bread – omit the pepper and stir in 1 teaspoon of sugar instead.

PER SERVING: 472 KCALS | 14.1G FAT | 4.6G SAT FAT | 58.9G CARBS | 13.7G SUGARS | 10.9G FIBRE | 27.6G PROTEIN | 0.6G SALT

BLACK RICE AND POMEGRANATE BOWL

This colourful bowl is full of flavour and bursting with protein-rich butter beans, black rice and cottage cheese. Kale and butternut squash also provide antioxidants to keep you happy and healthy.

SERVES: 4

PREP: 15 MINS   COOK: 25 MINS

1 small butternut squash, deseeded and diced
1 red onion, peeled and sliced
1 tbsp olive oil
125 g/4½ oz black rice
70 g/2½ oz kale, shredded
2 tbsp pine nuts
1 x 400 g/14 oz can butter beans, drained and rinsed
4 tbsp cottage cheese, to serve
seeds from 1 pomegranate, to serve

DRESSING
4 tbsp tahini paste
juice of 1 lemon
1 garlic clove, crushed
2 tbsp extra virgin olive oil

1. Preheat the oven to 200° C/400° F/Gas Mark 6.

2. Place the butternut squash and onion on a roasting tray and drizzle with the olive oil. Roast in the preheated oven for 15 minutes.

3. Cook the rice according to the packet instructions.

4. Meanwhile, add the kale and pine nuts to the squash and roast for a further 10 minutes. Remove from the oven and toss in the butter beans.

5. To make the dressing, whisk the tahini, lemon juice, garlic and olive oil together in a small bowl. Set aside.

6. Drain the rice and divide between four warmed bowls. Spoon over the roasted vegetables and nuts, a dollop of cottage cheese and a sprinkling of pomegranate seeds.

7. Drizzle the dressing into each bowl to serve.

VITAMIN C BOOST
For even more colour and extra vitamin C, add red and yellow peppers to the roasting tray with the squash.

PER SERVING: 492 KCALS | 23.7G FAT | 3.3G SAT FAT | 58.7G CARBS | 10.7G SUGARS | 10.5G FIBRE | 14.8G PROTEIN | 0.2G SALT

CHICKPEA TOFU STICKS WITH SPICY DIP

Cottage cheese is a fresh curd that's drained but not pressed, so some of the whey remains. As the base of a spicy dip, it tastes amazing dunked over strips of homemade tofu.

SERVES: 4
PREP: 15 MINS, PLUS STANDING AND CHILLING
COOK: 5–6 MINS

90 g/3¼ oz gram flour
1 tsp miso paste
½ tsp ground turmeric
500 ml/18 fl oz water

SPICY DIP
300 g/10½ oz cottage cheese
1 tbsp mayonnaise
2 tsp creamed horseradish
½ tsp Dijon mustard
1 spring onion, trimmed and finely chopped
12 olives, stoned and finely chopped

1. To make the chickpea tofu, place the gram flour in a bowl with the miso paste and turmeric. Whisk in 250 ml/9 fl oz of the water.

2. Bring the remaining water to the boil in a saucepan. When the water is boiling, pour the gram flour mix into the pan and start whisking.

3. Simmer while stirring constantly, until the mixture thickens. Pour it into a 15–cm/6–inch square tin or dish. Leave to stand at room temperature for 20 minutes, then chill in the fridge for at least 30 minutes.

4. Meanwhile, make the dip by combining the ingredients in a small bowl.

5. Cut the tofu into strips and serve with the spicy dip.

SPEEDY DIP
For a really quick dip, stir pesto through cottage cheese and top with Parmesan cheese shavings.

PER SERVING: 208 KCALS | 8.9G FAT | 1.9G SAT FAT | 18.7G CARBS | 5.9G SUGARS | 3.2G FIBRE | 13.3G PROTEIN | 1.1G SALT

RAW NUTTY PROTEIN BALLS

*These moreish little balls are the perfect post-exercise snack.
The assorted nuts and seeds provide lots of protein and minerals
while the glucose from the dried fruit replenishes energy levels.*

MAKES: 16 BALLS
PREP: 6 MINS, PLUS CHILLING   COOK: NONE

100 g/3½ oz ground almonds
100 g/3½ oz cashew nuts
40 g/1½ oz dried apricots
50 g/1¾ oz dried dates, stoned
seeds from ½ vanilla pod
20 g/¾ oz chia seeds
20 g/¾ oz coconut oil, melted

1. Place the ground almonds, cashew nuts, apricots, dates, vanilla seeds and chia seeds in a food processor and blitz until completely broken down.

2. With the machine running, pour in the coconut oil and blitz until the mixture starts to come together.

3. Roll the mixture into 16 balls using your hands. Place them on a plate and chill in the fridge for at least 30 minutes.

UP THE ANTI
For a treat and extra antioxidants, cover the balls in melted dark chocolate before popping them in the fridge.

PER BALL: 103 KCALS | 7.7G FAT | 1.8G SAT FAT | 7.5G CARBS | 4.1G SUGARS | 1.6G FIBRE | 2.8G PROTEIN | TRACE SALT

PINK
ENERGY BARS

The fun hidden ingredient in these bars is beetroot! Beetroot is an excellent source of folate and is full of magnesium, fibre, vitamin C, iron, vitamin B6, manganese, potassium and copper – a bundle of goodness!

MAKES: 10 BARS
PREP: 6 MINS, PLUS CHILLING   COOK: NONE

50 g/1¾ oz rolled oats
50 g/1¾ oz ground almonds
2 tbsp smooth peanut butter
1 small cooked beetroot
1 tbsp maple syrup

1. Place the oats in a food processor and blitz until broken down.

2. Add the remaining ingredients to the processor and blitz again until the mixture comes together.

3. Press the mixture into a 13–cm/5–inch square tin and smooth the top. Chill in the fridge for 1 hour, then cut into bars.

SWEET ENOUGH?
If you're in the mood for something a little less sweet, omit the maple syrup and add salt and pepper instead.

PER BAR: 76 KCALS | 4.6G FAT | 0.6G SAT FAT | 7.1G CARBS | 2.4G SUGARS | 1.4G FIBRE | 2.6G PROTEIN | TRACE SALT

NUT AND BERRY BARS

You can eat these bars for breakfast, a mid-afternoon snack or after-dinner sweet. The black treacle oozes with iron, calcium and magnesium, and the goji berries contain protein and fibre.

MAKES: 12 BARS
PREP: 12 MINS   COOK: 24–26 MINS

10 g/¼ oz butter, for greasing
100 g/3½ oz coconut oil
90 g/3¼ oz black treacle
20 g/¾ oz light muscovado sugar
20 g/¾ oz agave syrup
235 g/8½ oz rolled oats
10 g /¼ oz milk powder
50 g/1¾ oz pecan nuts, roughly chopped
30 g/1 oz Brazil nuts, roughly chopped
20 g/¾ oz goji berries

1. Preheat the oven to 180°C/350°F/Gas Mark 4. Grease an 18-cm/7-inch square tin and set aside.

2. In a large pan, melt the coconut oil over a medium heat with the treacle, sugar and agave syrup. Stir until the sugar has dissolved.

3. Pour the remaining ingredients into the pan and mix together well.

4. Pour the mixture into the prepared tin and level the top.

5. Bake for 18–20 minutes in the preheated oven. Remove from the oven and leave to cool completely before cutting into squares.

WHY NOT TRY?
Goji berries are available from most supermarkets and health food shops, but you can substitute them with dried cranberries, which are also great in flavour.

PER BAR: 242 KCALS | 14.9G FAT | 8.2G SAT FAT | 23.5G CARBS | 9.1G SUGARS | 2.8G FIBRE | 4G PROTEIN | TRACE SALT

ORANGE PROTEIN BARS

Chickpeas are rich in protein, full of fibre and provide essential minerals, such as potassium, which is important for preventing muscle cramps. Mixed with zesty orange rind, they make delicious snack bars.

MAKES: 10 BARS
PREP: 12 MINS, PLUS CHILLING   COOK: NONE

10 g/¼ oz butter, for greasing
1 x 400 g/14 oz can chickpeas, drained and rinsed
7 dates, stoned
1 tbsp ground linseeds
2 tbsp almond butter
½ tsp ground cinnamon
grated rind of 1 orange
2 tbsp chopped mixed peel

1. Grease and line the base of a 15–cm/6-inch square tin with non-stick kitchen paper. Set aside.

2. Place the chickpeas, dates, linseeds, almond butter, cinnamon and orange rind in a food processor and blitz until the mixture breaks down and starts to come together.

3. Stir the mixed peel into the processor.

4. Spoon the mixture into the prepared tin and smooth the top. Chill in the fridge for 1 hour, then remove from the tin and cut into bars.

LOVELY LINSEEDS
Linseeds are naturally gluten-free, a rich source of omega-3 essential fatty acids and a good source of fibre.

PER BAR: 83 KCALS | 3.4G FAT | 0.8G SAT FAT | 10.8G CARBS | 5.9G SUGARS | 2.7G FIBRE | 2.4G PROTEIN | 0.1G SALT

MAINS

WHOLEMEAL LINGUINE WITH MARINATED TOFU

Tofu is a soya-based protein that can be used in stir-fries and other vegetarian dishes. It doesn't have a strong flavour, so making a marinade with garlic, honey and chilli makes it even tastier.

SERVES: 4

PREP: 15 MINS, PLUS MARINATING   COOK: 15 MINS

175 g/6 oz tofu, cut into cubes (drained weight)
350 g/12 oz wholemeal linguine
1 tbsp olive oil, for frying
125 g/4½ oz chestnut mushrooms, sliced
2 fresh thyme sprigs, leaves only
juice of ½ lemon
salt and pepper (optional)
2 tbsp chopped fresh parsley, to garnish
2 tbsp freshly grated Parmesan cheese, to garnish

MARINADE
1 tbsp olive oil
juice and zest of ½ lime
1 garlic clove, crushed
¼ tsp chilli flakes
2 tbsp soy sauce
2 tbsp honey

1. To make the marinade, mix all the marinade ingredients together in a large bowl. Add the cubes of tofu, making sure each piece is coated in the mixture. Leave to marinate for at least 30 minutes.

2. Cook the linguine according to the packet instructions.

3. Meanwhile, heat the olive oil in a frying pan and cook the mushrooms for 5–6 minutes over a medium heat. Toss in the thyme leaves and lemon juice just before removing from the heat.

4. Heat a griddle pan until hot and cook the tofu over a medium heat for 5–6 minutes, until golden.

5. Drain the pasta and tip it into a large bowl with the mushroom mixture and tofu. Season to taste with salt and pepper, if using. Toss together.

6. Serve the pasta garnished with chopped parsley and grated cheese.

MARVELLOUS MUSHROOMS
Mushrooms are an ideal source of healthy protein for vegetarians and vegans.

PER SERVING: 463 KCALS | 12.2G FAT | 2G SAT FAT | 77.6G CARBS | 12.3G SUGARS | 8.7G FIBRE | 18.1G PROTEIN | 1.2G SALT

SALMON QUINOA BURGERS

Made with salmon, quinoa and egg, these burgers are full of protein. Topped with spicy mayonnaise and a spritz of lime juice, you'll be hard-pressed to find a tastier burger.

SERVES: 4
PREP: 15 MINS, PLUS CHILLING   COOK: 20–25 MINS

125 g/4½ oz quinoa
275 g/9¾ oz cooked salmon, broken into flakes
1 egg, beaten
4 spring onions, trimmed and sliced
1 tbsp chopped fresh coriander
4 wholemeal burger buns
1 tbsp olive oil, for frying
30 g/1 oz fresh watercress sprigs
¼ cucumber, sliced
salt and pepper (optional)
4 lime wedges, to serve

SPICY MAYONNAISE
2 tbsp capers, chopped
4 tbsp mayonnaise
juice of ½ lime

1. Bring a large saucepan of water to the boil. Add the quinoa and boil for 8–10 minutes. Drain well.

2. Place the quinoa in a bowl with the salmon, egg, spring onions and coriander. Season to taste with salt and pepper, if using, and mix well.

3. With your hands, shape the mixture into four patties. Place them on a plate and chill in the fridge for 20 minutes.

4. Meanwhile, make the spicy mayonnaise. Mix the capers, mayonnaise and lime juice together in a small bowl. Set aside.

5. Halve and toast the burger buns.

6. Heat the olive oil in a frying pan and cook the patties over a medium heat for 4–5 minutes on each side, until golden.

7. Spread the spicy mayonnaise over the bottom burger halves with a few sprigs of watercress and some slices of cucumber. Top with the burgers and sandwich with the second bun halves.

8. Serve the burgers with lime wedges.

SUPER SALMON
Salmon is an excellent source of omega-3 fats, cancer-fighting selenium and vitamin B12, which help protect against heart disease and chronic diseases such as Alzheimer's disease, depression and diabetes.

PER SERVING: 542 KCALS | 27.3G FAT | 4.4G SAT FAT | 48.7G CARBS | 4.1G SUGARS | 4G FIBRE | 26.1G PROTEIN | 1.2G SALT

BUTTERNUT SQUASH AND LENTIL BOWL

Most plant-based foods do not include all the essential amino acids that make up protein in one ingredient, but lentils and rice will make a complete protein meal. To further increase the protein content, use all wild rice.

SERVES: 4
PREP: 10 MINS   COOK: 50 MINS

2 butternut squash
2 tbsp olive oil
150 g/5½ oz brown basmati and wild rice
1 tsp melted coconut oil
4 spring onions, trimmed and sliced
3–cm/1¼–inch piece fresh ginger, grated
1 lemon grass stalk, trimmed and finely sliced
1 tbsp Thai green curry paste
400 ml/14 fl oz canned coconut milk
400 g/14 oz canned green lentils
100 g/3½ oz cavolo nero, chopped
1 tbsp golden sesame seeds
1 tbsp black sesame seeds
10 g/¼ oz fresh coriander leaves, to garnish

1. Preheat the oven to 200°C/400°F/Gas Mark 6.

2. Halve the squash, scoop out the seeds and score the flesh with a sharp knife.

3. Place the four squash halves on a baking tray and drizzle with olive oil. Roast in the preheated oven for 40 minutes. Meanwhile, cook the rice according to the packet instructions.

4. While the rice is cooking, heat the coconut oil in a frying pan. Add the spring onions, ginger and lemon grass and cook for 1 minute, then stir in the curry paste and cook for a further minute.

5. Add the coconut milk and lentils and bring to the boil. Simmer for 15 minutes.

6. Drain the rice and add to the lentil mixture, with the cavolo nero. Simmer for 3–4 minutes.

7. Take the squash out of the oven and divide the lentil and rice mixture between the four halves.

8. Sprinkle with the sesame seeds and bake for a further 10 minutes. Sprinkle with the coriander leaves and serve.

DID YOU KNOW?
Cavolo nero is an Italian cabbage that has dark green leaves. If you can't find it you can always use its cousin kale instead.

PER SERVING: 626 KCALS | 33.5G FAT | 21.2G SAT FAT | 72.6G CARBS | 9.7G SUGARS | 11.6G FIBRE | 16.2G PROTEIN | 0.1G SALT

BAKED CHICKEN WITH PEARS AND HAZELNUTS

The combination of chicken and pears is an unusual one,
but it works very well in this easy and healthy supper.

SERVES: 4

PREP: 15 MINS   COOK: 30 MINS

4 skinless chicken breast fillets,
each weighing about 140 g/5 oz
1½ tbsp extra virgin rapeseed oil
4 large shallots, cut into quarters
2 small pears, peeled, cored and quartered
100 ml/3½ fl oz dry white wine
2 tsp garlic purée
2 tsp dried oregano
100 ml/3½ fl oz chicken stock
½ tsp salt
½ tsp pepper
40 g/1½ oz blanched hazelnuts, finely chopped
2 tbsp wholemeal breadcrumbs
2 tbsp chopped fresh parsley
2 tsp fresh thyme leaves

1. Preheat the oven to 180° C/350° F/Gas Mark 4. Cut each of the chicken breasts into two thick steaks.

2. Place a large frying pan over a medium heat and add 1 tablespoon of the oil. Add the shallot quarters and fry for 5 minutes, or until soft and light golden. Set aside until required.

3. Add the chicken and pears to the pan and fry over a high heat for 2–3 minutes, turning once, until light golden (you may need to do this in two batches). Arrange the chicken in a large shallow baking dish, tucking the shallots and pears around the edge.

4. Add the wine to the pan and bring to the boil. Stir in half the garlic and all the oregano, then stir in the stock, salt and pepper. Pour the contents of the pan over the chicken mixture. Bake in the preheated oven for 15 minutes, basting the tops of the chicken pieces once or twice with the cooking juices.

5. Meanwhile, combine the hazelnuts, breadcrumbs, parsley and thyme with the remaining oil and garlic in a small bowl. Sprinkle the mixture over the top of the chicken and return to the oven for 10 minutes, or until the top has crisped a little and is lightly golden, and the chicken is tender and the juices run clear when a skewer is inserted into the thickest part of the meat. Serve immediately.

COOK'S TIP

This dish is good served with French beans and broccoli and also goes well with new potatoes in their skins.

PER SERVING: 350 KCALS | 15.3G FAT | 1.7G SAT FAT | 16.9G CARBS | 6.5G SUGARS | 3.7G FIBRE | 32.6G PROTEIN | 1.4G SALT

GRILLED CHICKEN AND SLAW BOWL

Here's a perfect mid-week meal for essential protein and energy: crunchy vegetables drizzled in a spicy mayonnaise and topped with tender slices of chicken.

SERVES: 4
PREP: 18 MINS   COOK: 8–10 MINS

4 x 150 g/5½ oz boneless, skinless chicken breasts
1 tsp smoked paprika
salt and pepper (optional)
12 fresh rocket leaves, to garnish

COLESLAW
2 carrots, peeled and grated
1 fennel bulb, trimmed and thinly sliced
1 beetroot, grated
150 g/5½ oz red cabbage, shredded
150 g/5½ oz white cabbage, shredded
4 radishes, thinly sliced
1 red onion, peeled and thinly sliced
15 g/½ oz fresh mixed herbs, such as parsley, dill, mint
and coriander, chopped
juice of 1 lemon
2 tbsp extra virgin olive oil
250 g/9 oz natural yogurt
1 tbsp wholegrain mustard

1. To make the coleslaw, place all the coleslaw ingredients together in a large bowl. Toss together really well and set aside.

2. Preheat the grill to a medium heat. Place the chicken breasts between two sheets of greaseproof paper and flatten with a rolling pin or mallet, to a thickness of 1–2 cm/½–¾ inch.

3. Season the chicken with paprika, and salt and pepper, if using. Grill for 4–5 minutes on each side, until the chicken is tender and the juices run clear when a skewer is inserted into the thickest part of the meat.

4. Divide the coleslaw between four bowls and top with slices of chicken breast and the rocket leaves.

DID YOU KNOW?
Flattening the chicken breasts helps them to cook more quickly and evenly. Remove the skin as this is where the fat is.

PER SERVING: 362 KCALS | 13.4G FAT | 3.1G SAT FAT | 21.9G CARBS | 12.7G SUGARS | 6.1G FIBRE | 39.2G PROTEIN | 0.5G SALT

LENTIL AND AMARANTH TABBOULEH

Amaranth is a high-quality source of plant protein, including the amino acids lysine and methionine. It's also bursting with iron and calcium, so it's an essential grain to have in your kitchen.

SERVES: 4

PREP: 25 MINS   COOK: 30 MINS

150 g/5½ oz amaranth
1 x 400 g/14 oz can green lentils, drained and rinsed
½ cucumber, diced
8 tomatoes, diced
1 small red onion, peeled and diced
15 g/½ oz fresh parsley, chopped
15 g/½ oz fresh mint, chopped
15 g/½ oz fresh coriander, chopped
100 g /3½ oz hazelnuts, toasted and chopped
150 g/5½ oz halloumi cheese, thickly sliced
salt and pepper (optional)
seeds from 1 pomegranate, to garnish
2 tbsp coconut flakes, to garnish
2 tbsp avocado oil, to serve

DRESSING
3 tbsp olive oil
1 tbsp balsamic vinegar
1 tsp wholegrain mustard
1 tsp honey

1. Cook the amaranth according to the packet instructions, until the grains are fluffy. Drain and leave to cool for a few minutes.

2. Meanwhile, make the dressing. Whisk the olive oil, vinegar, mustard and honey together in a bowl.

3. Place the amaranth in a large bowl with the lentils, cucumber, tomatoes, onion, herbs and hazelnuts. Pour over the dressing and toss together. Season to taste with salt and pepper, if using, and leave to stand at room temperature.

4. In a dry frying pan, cook the halloumi over a medium heat, until golden on both sides.

5. Serve the halloumi with the tabbouleh, garnished with pomegranate seeds, coconut flakes and a drizzle of avocado oil.

HELPFUL HAZELNUTS
Hazelnuts are a good source of protein and monounsaturated fats. They are also very rich in the antioxidant vitamin E.

PER SERVING: 727 KCALS | 47.1G FAT | 10.9G SAT FAT | 57.8G CARBS | 17.1G SUGARS | 12.8G FIBRE | 23.5G PROTEIN | 1.2G SALT

ONE-PAN SPICY CHICKEN

*This dish is based on the gorgeous stews made in Morocco,
using fruits (apricots in this instance, which are rich in iron)
to add sweetness and a combination of spices for a fragrant sauce.*

SERVES: 4
PREP: 15 MINS   COOK: 30–35 MINS

2 onions, peeled
100 g/3½ oz tomatoes, halved
3–cm/1¼–inch piece fresh ginger, peeled and chopped
3 garlic cloves, peeled
2 tbsp olive oil
4 x 150 g/5½ oz boneless, skinless chicken breasts, cut
into bite–sized pieces
2 tsp ground cinnamon
1 tsp ground turmeric
2 tsp ground cumin
2 tsp ground coriander
1 large butternut squash, deseeded and cut into large
pieces
50 g/1¾ oz dried apricots, halved
600 ml/1 pint chicken stock
175 g/6 oz red quinoa
125 g/4½ oz feta cheese, crumbled
salt and pepper (optional)
15 g/½ oz fresh mint leaves, chopped, to garnish

1. Chop 1 of the onions and place in a blender with the tomatoes, ginger and garlic. Blitz to a paste.

2. Heat the olive oil in a large pan or casserole and cook the chicken over a medium heat for 4–5 minutes, until browned all over. Remove from the pan and reserve.

3. Slice the remaining onion and cook in the same pan over a medium heat for 3–4 minutes, then stir in the spices and cook for a further minute.

4. Stir the onion and tomato paste into the pan and cook for 2 minutes.

5. Return the chicken to the pan with the squash, apricots and stock. Simmer for 15–20 minutes, until the chicken is cooked through. Season to taste with salt and pepper, if using.

6. Meanwhile, cook the quinoa according to the packet instructions.

7. Divide the chicken mixture and quinoa between four serving plates and sprinkle with feta and mint to serve.

WHY NOT TRY?
Other types of meat can be cooked this way – the recipe works perfectly with pork loin, for example.

PER SERVING: 656 KCALS | 21.6G FAT | 7.2G SAT FAT | 71.3G CARBS | 15.6G SUGARS | 10.9G FIBRE | 48.5G PROTEIN | 2.2G SALT

QUINOA CHILLI

Quinoa is a South American grain that contains all nine essential amino acids. It's easy to cook and is a great, wheat-free replacement to rice or couscous.

SERVES: 4
PREP: 12 MINS   COOK: 36 MINS

50 g/1³⁄₄ oz red quinoa
1 tbsp olive oil, for sautéing
1 onion, peeled and diced
2 green chillies, deseeded and diced
1¹⁄₂ tsp smoked paprika
1 tsp chilli powder
2 tsp cumin powder
¹⁄₂ tsp cayenne pepper
2 garlic cloves, crushed
2 x 400 g/14 oz can chopped tomatoes
1 x 400 g/14 oz can kidney beans, drained and rinsed
1 x 400 g/14 oz cans flageolet beans, drained and rinsed
100 ml/3¹⁄₂ fl oz water
15 g/¹⁄₂ oz fresh coriander leaves, chopped
2 tbsp frozen sweetcorn kernels, thawed
2 tbsp soured cream, to serve

1. Cook the quinoa according to the packet instructions.

2. Meanwhile, heat the oil in a separate large pan and sauté the onion over a medium heat for 3–4 minutes to soften.

3. Add the chillies to the pan and cook for 1 minute. Stir in the spices and garlic, and cook for 1 minute more.

4. Drain the quinoa and add to the pan along with the tomatoes, beans and water. Bring to a simmer and cook for 30 minutes, stirring occasionally, until thickened. Stir in half the coriander leaves.

5. Divide the chilli between four warmed serving bowls and scatter the sweetcorn kernels and remaining coriander over the top. Serve with the soured cream.

BRILLIANT BEANS

Kidney beans are an excellent source of protein, iron and calcium for vegetarians and vegans. An average portion of kidney beans contains at least a quarter of our day's iron needs to help prevent anaemia and increase energy levels, while their good zinc content helps boost the immune system.

PER SERVING: 277 KCALS | 7.4G FAT | 1.3G SAT FAT | 38.6G CARBS | 10.5G SUGARS | 9.6G FIBRE | 12.3G PROTEIN | 0.1G SALT

TURKEY, SESAME AND GINGER NOODLES

Turkey is one of the leanest meats you can buy and an invaluable source of protein. Unlike other meats, it also has a high amount of tryptophan, which can act as a mood stabilizer.

SERVES: 4
PREP: 10 MINS   COOK: 12 MINS

150 g/5½ oz egg noodles
1 tbsp olive oil, for frying
2 garlic cloves, crushed
3–cm/1¼–inch piece fresh root ginger,
peeled and diced
400 g/14 oz turkey breast, cut into strips
125 g/4½ oz mangetout
100 g/3½ oz broccoli florets
1 red pepper, deseeded and sliced
2 spring onions, trimmed and sliced
150 g/5½ oz beansprouts
1 tbsp sesame oil
1 tbsp soy sauce
1 tbsp sweet chilli sauce
juice of ½ lime
100 g/3½ oz smooth peanut butter
100 g/3½ oz roasted peanuts, chopped
15 g/½ oz fresh coriander leaves, to garnish

1. Cook the egg noodles according to the packet instructions.

2. Heat the olive oil in a wok or large frying pan and add the garlic, ginger and turkey. Stir–fry over a medium heat for 3–4 minutes, until the turkey is cooked through. Remove from the pan and reserve.

3. Add the mangetout, broccoli and red pepper to the wok and stir–fry over a medium heat for 4–5 minutes. Add the spring onions and beansprouts, and continue to cook for 1 minute.

4. Whisk the sesame oil, soy sauce, chilli sauce, lime juice and peanut butter together in a small bowl and add to the wok along with the turkey and noodles. Toss together really well.

5. Divide the turkey and noodles between four warmed serving bowls and top with the peanuts and coriander to serve.

COOK'S TIP
This dish is delicious eaten hot or cold. Take any leftovers to work the next day for an easy lunch.

PER SERVING: 675 KCALS | 35.6G FAT | 6.2G SAT FAT | 50.2G CARBS | 11.5G SUGARS | 7.8G FIBRE | 44.2G PROTEIN | 1.3G SALT

BULGUR WHEAT BALLS WITH CHICKPEA HUMMUS

These vegetarian 'wheat balls' are just as delicious as the meat variety. Made from bulgur wheat and served with a velvety chickpea and walnut hummus, this is a nutritious family meal.

SERVES: 4
PREP: 20 MINS, PLUS CHILLING   COOK: 25–30 MINS

200 g/7 oz bulgur wheat
1 small red onion, peeled and diced
2 tsp ground cumin
2 tsp ground turmeric
½ tsp smoked paprika
15 g/½ oz fresh coriander, chopped
2 eggs, beaten
2 tbsp olive oil, for frying
2 tbsp sesame seeds, toasted, to garnish
4 small handfuls fresh watercress
(about 15 g/½ oz each), to serve

CHICKPEA HUMMUS
1 x 400 g/14 oz can chickpeas, drained and rinsed
60 g/2¼ oz walnuts, toasted
1 garlic clove, crushed
juice of 1 lemon
7 tbsp extra virgin olive oil
salt and pepper (optional)

1. Bring a large saucepan of water to the boil. Add the bulgur wheat and cook for 20 minutes, until very soft. Drain and refresh under cold running water.

2. In a bowl, mix the bulgur wheat, onion, spices, coriander and eggs together.

3. Shape the mixture into 12 walnut-sized balls using your hands. Place them on a plate and chill in the fridge for 30 minutes.

4. Meanwhile, make the hummus. Place the chickpeas and walnuts in a food processor and blitz until they resemble breadcrumbs.

5. Add the garlic and lemon juice to the processor and blitz again.

6. With the machine running, gradually add the extra virgin olive oil until you have a smooth consistency. Season to taste with salt and pepper, if using. Transfer the hummus to a bowl and set aside.

7. Heat the olive oil in a frying pan and cook the balls over a medium heat for 3–4 minutes, occasionally turning them to brown all over.

8. Serve the bulgur wheat balls on a bed of watercress, topped with a dollop of hummus and sprinkled with toasted sesame seeds.

WHY NOT TRY?
For another great hummus recipe, swap the walnuts for a peeled and chopped avocado – it tastes heavenly and is full of healthy fats.

PER SERVING: 700 KCALS | 46.3G FAT | 6G SAT FAT | 55.1G CARBS | 4.4G SUGARS | 14.7G FIBRE | 18.3G PROTEIN | 0.2G SALT

PAN-FRIED TUNA WITH SEAWEED PESTO

You may associate seaweed with Japanese cuisine, but it's actually a very versatile ingredient. It's highly nutritious and one of the few ingredients that's rich in iodine, which is important for thyroid health.

SERVES: 4
PREP: 20 MINS COOK: 25 MINS

4 x 150 g/5½ oz tuna steaks
4 tsp black pepper
1 tbsp olive oil
4 small handfuls fresh watercress
(about 15 g/½ oz each)

SWEET POTATO WEDGES

2 sweet potatoes, cut into wedges
3 tbsp olive oil
¼ tsp smoked paprika
salt and pepper (optional)

SEAWEED PESTO

30 g/1 oz dried wakame, soaked in water for 20 minutes
until rehydrated, drained
½ garlic clove, chopped
20 g/¾ oz pine nuts, toasted
15 g/½ oz pecorino cheese, grated
juice of ½ lemon
90 ml/3 fl oz extra virgin olive oil

1. Preheat the oven to 200°C/400°F/Gas Mark 6.

2. To make the sweet potato wedges, toss the sweet potato wedges in a bowl with the olive oil and paprika. Season to taste with salt and pepper, if using, then spread across a baking sheet or roasting tray.

3. Roast the sweet potato in the preheated oven for 15–20 minutes, until tender.

4. Meanwhile, make the seaweed pesto. Place the rehydrated wakame in a food processor with the garlic and pine nuts, and process to break down.

5. Add the cheese and lemon juice to the processor and pulse again.

6. With the machine running, slowly add the extra virgin olive oil until you have a pesto consistency. Transfer to a bowl and set aside.

7. Season each tuna steak with 1 teaspoon of black pepper. Make sure both sides are seasoned.

8. Heat the olive oil in a pan and cook the tuna over a high heat for 3–4 minutes on each side, depending on how pink you like it.

9. Serve the pan-fried tuna with a dollop of seaweed pesto, the sweet potato wedges and watercress.

SWEET POTATO POWER
Sweet potatoes are richer in nutrients than potatoes and lower on the glycaemic index.

PER SERVING: 602 KCALS | 41.4G FAT | 6G SAT FAT | 17.1G CARBS | 3.1G SUGARS | 2.8G FIBRE | 40.2G PROTEIN | 0.6G SALT

MIXED BEAN, NUT AND KALE STEW

Kale is a wonderfully nourishing vegetable, rich in vitamin B6, fibre, potassium, magnesium and more. Served with protein-packed beans, this is a dinner the entire family will enjoy.

SERVES: 4
PREP: 10 MINS COOK: 30 MINS

1 tbsp olive oil, for sautéing
1 large onion, peeled and chopped
2 garlic cloves, peeled and sliced
1 tsp smoked paprika
200 g/7 oz broad beans
1 x 400 g/14 oz can butter beans, drained and rinsed
100 g/3½ oz green beans, trimmed and halved
1 x 400 g/14 oz can chopped tomatoes
200 ml/7 fl oz vegetable stock
150 g/5½ oz kale, shredded
2 tbsp walnuts, chopped
1 tbsp Brazil nuts, chopped
1 tbsp hazelnuts, chopped
175 g/6 oz feta cheese, crumbled
salt and pepper (optional)
1 tbsp chopped fresh mint, to garnish
1 tbsp extra virgin olive oil, to serve

1. Heat the olive oil in a large pan and sauté the onion over a medium heat for 2–3 minutes. Stir in the garlic and paprika, and cook for a further minute.

2. Stir the beans, tomatoes and stock into the pan and bring to a simmer. Cook for 15 minutes, then stir in the kale and cook for a further 10 minutes. Season to taste with salt and pepper, if using.

3. Toast the nuts in a dry pan over a medium heat for 2–3 minutes.

4. Ladle the stew into four bowls and serve topped with the toasted nuts, feta, chopped mint and a drizzle of olive oil.

COOK'S TIP
If you can get broad beans in season, these are preferable. If not, substitute with frozen broad beans.

PER SERVING: 408 KCALS | 23.1G FAT | 8.4G SAT FAT | 30.5G CARBS | 9.7G SUGARS | 10.1G FIBRE | 19.5G PROTEIN | 1.5G SALT

MISO STEAK AND PEPPER STIR-FRY

Steak is high in protein but also contains saturated fat, so it's important to pick really lean cuts and not eat red meat too often. Instead, try to fill up on different fish and vegetables.

SERVES: 4
PREP: 15 MINS, PLUS CHILLING   COOK: 15 MINS

350 g/12 oz lean beef steaks
1 tbsp melted coconut oil, for frying
4 spring onions, cut into 4-cm/1½-inch lengths
2-cm/¾-inch piece fresh root ginger, peeled and grated
1 carrot, peeled and cut into matchsticks
1 red pepper, deseeded and sliced
1 yellow pepper, deseeded and sliced
100 g/3½ oz baby sweetcorn, halved
1 courgette, cut into matchsticks
100 g/3½ oz mangetout, shredded
1 tbsp soy sauce
2 tbsp sesame seeds, to garnish

MARINADE
2 tbsp brown miso paste
1 tbsp sake
1 tbsp caster sugar
2 garlic cloves, crushed

1. To make the marinade, mix the marinade ingredients together in a non-metallic bowl. Add the steaks and rub all over with the mixture. Cover and chill in the fridge for at least 1 hour (the longer the better).

2. Heat a griddle pan and cook the steaks over a medium heat for 2–3 minutes on each side, depending on how pink you like your steak. Remove from the pan and leave to rest.

3. Meanwhile, heat the coconut oil in a wok or large frying pan and cook the spring onions and ginger over a medium heat for 2 minutes.

4. Add the carrot, peppers and sweetcorn to the wok and stir-fry for 2 minutes, then add the courgette and mangetout. Stir-fry for a further 3 minutes.

5. Slice the steaks and add to the wok with the soy sauce. Stir-fry for 1 minute, until all the vegetables are cooked but not soft.

6. Divide the steak slices and vegetables between four plates and sprinkle with sesame seeds. Serve immediately.

PROTECTIVE PEPPERS
The bright colours of peppers contain high levels of carotenes for heart health and cancer protection, and are also a rich source of vitamin C.

PER SERVING: 260 KCALS | 9.1G FAT | 4.2G SAT FAT | 18.5G CARBS | 11.2G SUGARS | 4.5G FIBRE | 26.2G PROTEIN | 1.5G SALT

DESSERTS AND BAKING

BLACK RICE PUDDING WITH GINGER AND PINEAPPLE

Black rice turns a classic pudding into a stylish, contemporary dish. A great source of iron, vitamin E and antioxidants, it's also higher in fibre and protein than white or brown rice.

SERVES: 4

PREP: 8 MINS   COOK: 25 MINS

175 g/6 oz black rice
100 ml/3½ fl oz soya single cream
225 g/8 oz fresh pineapple, halved
6 knobs stem ginger, diced
4 tbsp stem ginger syrup
15 g/½ oz fresh mint leaves, shredded
4 tbsp coconut yogurt

1. Cook the rice according to the packet instructions.

2. Drain the rice and place three quarters of it in a food processor with the soya cream and half the pineapple. Blitz until you have the consistency of rice pudding.

3. Spoon the rice mixture into four glasses.

4. Dice the remaining pineapple and place in a bowl with the diced ginger, syrup and mint. Mix well.

5. Spoon the coconut yogurt over the rice mixture, then pour over the ginger and pineapple mixture to serve.

PERFECT PINEAPPLE

Pineapples are a good source of vitamin C and other vitamins and minerals, including magnesium.

PER SERVING: 277 KCALS | 6.9G FAT | 3.2G SAT FAT | 48.3G CARBS | 15.3G SUGARS | 3G FIBRE | 5.7G PROTEIN | TRACE SALT

MATCHA CASHEW CREAM TARTS

Matcha is a stone-ground green tea traditionally used in Japanese tea ceremonies. Aside from its various vitamins and minerals, it's valued for polyphenol compounds called catechins – antioxidants that help fight disease.

MAKES: 8 TARTS
PREP: 20 MINS, PLUS CHILLING   COOK: NONE

75 g/2¾ oz coconut oil, melted, plus 1 tbsp for oiling
6 dates, stoned
50 g/1¾ oz coconut flour
75 g/2¾ oz desiccated coconut
20 g/¾ oz ground almonds
1 tsp matcha powder

CASHEW CREAM

100 g/3½ oz cashew nuts, soaked in boiling water for 15 minutes, drained and rinsed
50 ml/2 fl oz water
1 tbsp maple syrup
2 tbsp natural yogurt
1 banana, peeled and sliced
2 passion fruits, pulp only, to decorate

1. Oil an 8-hole muffin tin with coconut oil and line with paper cases. Set aside.

2. Pour the melted coconut oil into a food processor with the dates, coconut flour, desiccated coconut, ground almonds and matcha powder. Process until the mixture is well combined.

3. Divide the mixture between the cases in your prepared tin and press down, making little tarts. Chill in the fridge for at least 1 hour.

4. Meanwhile, make your cashew cream. Place the soaked nuts in a food processor with the water and maple syrup. Blend until just combined.

5. Add the yogurt and half the banana slices to the processor and continue to blend until smooth.

6. Remove the chilled tarts from the tin and spoon a dollop of the cashew cream onto each one. Decorate each tart with a few slices of banana and a little passion fruit pulp.

GOOD-FOR-YOU CASHEWS
High in monounsaturated fats, cashew nuts help protect the heart, and contain a range of minerals for strong bones, improved immunity and increased energy levels.

PER TART: 293 KCALS | 23.3G FAT | 15.2G SAT FAT | 18.2G CARBS | 10.2G SUGARS | 5.5G FIBRE | 5G PROTEIN | TRACE SALT

FROZEN YOGURT BARK

*If you're struggling to think of healthy treats for your children,
this frozen yogurt dessert makes a great after-school snack and will
replace crisps and sweets with an assortment of fruits and nuts.*

SERVES: 4

PREP: 10 MINS, PLUS FREEZING   COOK: NONE

500 g/1 lb 2 oz Greek-style yogurt
2 tbsp maple syrup
zest of 1 orange
50 g/1³/₄ oz blueberries
50 g/1³/₄ oz dried cherries
100 g/3¹/₂ oz pistachio nuts, roughly chopped
100 g/3¹/₂ oz raspberries

1. Line a 16 x 26-cm/6¹/₄ x 10¹/₂-inch shallow tin with non-stick baking paper, leaving extra paper hanging over the rim (this will help you lift the bark out once frozen). Set aside.

2. Place the yogurt, maple syrup, orange zest, blueberries and cherries in a large bowl and mix together.

3. Pour the yogurt mixture into the prepared tin and make sure the fruit is evenly dispersed.

4. Sprinkle the chopped pistachio nuts and raspberries on top of the yogurt. Freeze for at least 2 hours, or until completely frozen.

5. Remove the bark from the tin with the overhanging pieces of paper and cut into shapes of your choice.

INCREASED POWER
To increase the protein content, you could stir
some nut butter through the yogurt.

PER SERVING: 349 KCALS | 17.9G FAT | 6G SAT FAT | 33.4G CARBS | 23.5G SUGARS | 5G FIBRE | 16.9G PROTEIN | 0.1G SALT

NO-BAKE BERRY CHEESECAKE

There's no baking required for this beautiful cheesecake – just pop it in the fridge! Different toppings can be added – try mango and passion fruit, oranges and stemmed ginger, or pomegranate and pistachio.

SERVES: 8

PREP: 20 MINS, PLUS CHILLING   COOK: NONE

1 tbsp melted coconut oil, for oiling
50 g/1³/₄ oz walnuts
60 g/2¹/₄ oz ground almonds
200 g/7 oz Medjool dates, stoned
1 tbsp melted coconut oil

FILLING

600 g/1 lb 5 oz cream cheese
grated zest of 2 lemons
100 g/3¹/₂ oz icing sugar
100 ml/3¹/₂ fl oz double cream
200 g/7 oz Greek-style yogurt

TOPPING

100 g/3¹/₂ oz blueberries
100 g/3¹/₂ oz raspberries
100 g/3¹/₂ oz strawberries
1 tbsp cacao nibs, to decorate (optional)
15 g/¹/₂ oz fresh mint leaves, to decorate

1. Lightly oil a 23-cm/9-inch springform tin with coconut oil and set aside.

2. Place the walnuts, ground almonds and dates in a food processor and blitz until they are broken down to a fine crumb. While the machine is running, pour in the second tablespoon of coconut oil.

3. Press the base mixture into the bottom of the prepared tin.

4. To make the filling, place the cream cheese, lemon zest and icing sugar in a bowl and, using a hand whisk, whisk until smooth. Add the cream and yogurt, and continue to whisk until the mixture is combined and stiff.

5. Spoon the cream cheese filling onto the base and chill in the fridge for at least 3 hours.

6. Remove the cheesecake from the tin and place on a serving plate. Sprinkle over the blueberries and raspberries.

7. Purée the strawberries in a small blender and drizzle over the top of the cheesecake. Decorate with mint leaves and cacao nibs, if using, to serve.

MAKE IT CHOCOLATEY

To make a no-bake chocolate cheesecake, add 1 tablespoon of cocoa powder to the base and swirl 150 g/5¹/₂ oz melted dark chocolate over the top before sprinkling with mint and cacao nibs.

PER SERVING: 593 KCALS | 44.6G FAT | 23.4G SAT FAT | 43.5G CARBS | 35.9G SUGARS | 4.5G FIBRE | 10.5G PROTEIN | 0.6G SALT

CHOCOLATE YOGURT POPS

Instead of buying sugar-laden lollies, make these naturally sweet chocolate yogurt pops. They'll be a huge success on hot summer days.

MAKES: 10 POPS
PREP: 20 MINS, PLUS FREEZING COOK: NONE

325 g/11½ oz Greek-style yogurt
2 bananas, peeled and mashed
4 tsp honey
300 g /10½ oz dark chocolate, chopped
100 g/3½ oz coconut oil
100 g/3½ oz milk chocolate, chopped
100 g/3½ oz white chocolate, chopped
1 tbsp pistachio nuts, chopped

YOU WILL ALSO NEED:
10 x 100 ml/3½ fl oz ice lolly moulds
10 ice lolly sticks

1. Place the yogurt in a bowl with the mashed banana and honey. Mix well.

2. Pour the yogurt mixture into 10 x 100 ml/3½ fl oz lolly moulds. Insert the ice lolly sticks and freeze for at least 2 hours.

3. Gently melt the dark chocolate and coconut oil in a heatproof bowl suspended over a pan of simmering water. Don't let the bowl touch the water.

4. Melt the milk chocolate in the same way as the dark chocolate.

5. Remove the lollies from their moulds and dip into the melted dark chocolate and coconut oil, then return to the freezer for a couple of minutes to set.

6. To decorate the lollies, swirl milk chocolate around each one with a fork, then sprinkle with white chocolate and pistachio nuts. Return to the freezer to set.

DID YOU KNOW?
Bananas are antacids, lowering the distress associated with heartburn, stomach aches and acid reflux.

PER POP: 438 KCALS | 29.7G FAT | 19.9G SAT FAT | 36.7G CARBS | 28.5G SUGARS | 3.5G FIBRE | 6.5G PROTEIN | 0.1G SALT

CHOCOLATE AND CHIA PUDDINGS

Coconut milk and natural yogurt add an appealing creaminess to these chilled chocolate puddings, plus agave syrup sweetens them naturally and on-trend chia seeds add that extra nutrient boost.

SERVES: 3
PREP: 20 MINS, PLUS CHILLING COOK: NONE

2 tbsp cocoa powder
2 tbsp agave syrup
90 ml/3 fl oz coconut milk
125 g/4½ oz Greek–style natural yogurt
2 tbsp chia seeds
1 tsp vanilla extract
1 kiwi, sliced, to decorate
50 g/1¾ oz plain chocolate, roughly chopped, to decorate

1: Place the cocoa powder and agave syrup in a large bowl and mix well to remove any lumps. Stir in the coconut milk, Greek yogurt, chia seeds and vanilla extract and mix thoroughly.

2: Cover and refrigerate for 4–6 hours. Remove the mixture from the refrigerator; it should be quite thick at this stage. Using an electric hand–held blender, whizz the mixture until smooth and carefully divide between three small dessert glasses.

3: Chill the puddings for a further hour. Decorate with the kiwi slices and plain chocolate and serve.

SKIN-SOOTHING KIWI
Kiwi fruit is full of omega–3, important in preventing an array of skin diseases and protecting the health of cell membranes. As a strong provider of vitamin C and vitamin E, it helps to maintain the skin's moisture and aids the healing of cuts and scars.

PER SERVING: 307 KCALS | 18.8G FAT | 11.8G SAT FAT | 29.7G CARBS | 18.7G SUGARS | 7G FIBRE | 7.9G PROTEIN | TRACE SALT

HEALTHY COOKIE DOUGH DIP

This cookie dough isn't what it seems! Mixing butter beans with dark chocolate and almond makes a delicious dip but without all the refined sugar and calories.

SERVES: 4
PREP: 8–10 MINS   COOK: NONE

1 x 400 g/14 oz can butter beans, drained and rinsed
½ tsp bicarbonate of soda
3 drops vanilla extract
2 tbsp almond butter
1 tbsp almond milk
1 tbsp ground linseeds
½ tsp honey, plus extra to taste (optional)
50 g/1¾ oz dark chocolate, chopped
sliced fresh fruits, such as banana, strawberries, pear, mango and melon, to serve (optional)

1. Place all the ingredients, except the chocolate, in a food processor and blitz until nearly smooth. Add a little more honey if you'd like the dip to be sweeter.

2. Stir the chopped chocolate into the dip and serve with the fruit of your choice, if using.

COOK'S TIP
You can use other white beans, or chickpeas,
if you don't have any butter beans.

PER SERVING: 198 KCALS | 10.4G FAT | 3.4G SAT FAT | 18.5G CARBS | 6.3G SUGARS | 5.4G FIBRE | 7.1G PROTEIN | 0.4G SALT

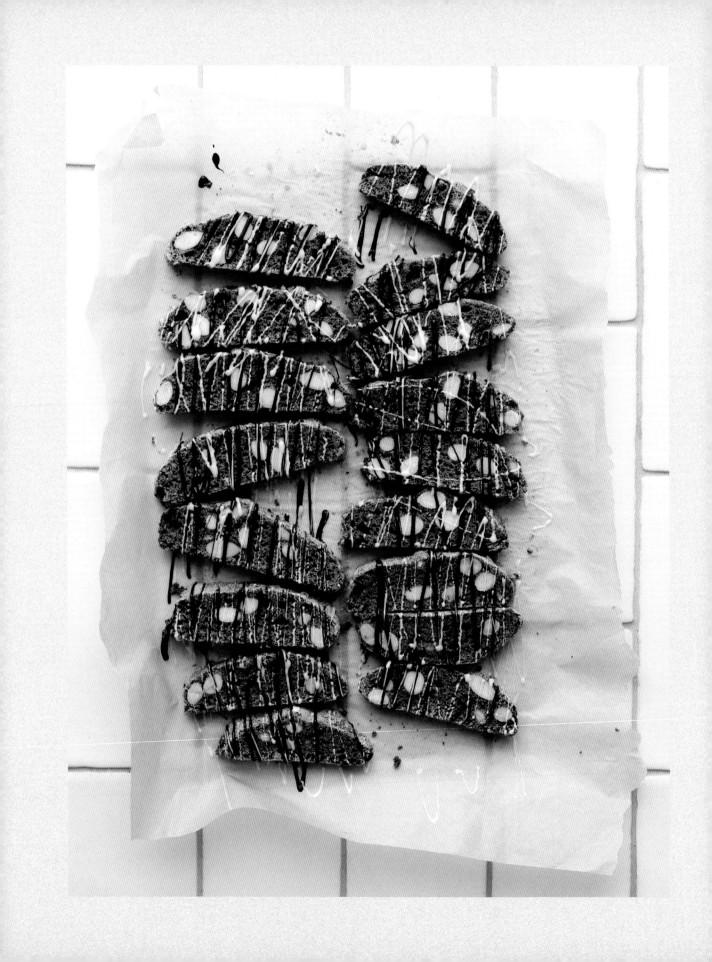

CHOCOLATE AND ALMOND BISCOTTI

Biscotti are Italian biscuits twice baked for a crunchy coating and traditionally served with coffee. These are made with almonds for protein, calcium and potassium and are decorated with chocolate drizzle.

MAKES: 22 BISCOTTI
PREP: 15 MINS   COOK: 50–60 MINS

1 tsp baking powder
150 g/5½ oz plain flour
90 g/3¼ oz buckwheat flour
150 g/5½ oz golden caster sugar
20 g/¾ oz cacao powder
¼ tsp ground cinnamon
4 eggs, beaten
175 g/6 oz blanched almonds, toasted and roughly chopped
100 g/3½ oz dark chocolate, to decorate
100 g/3½ oz white chocolate, to decorate

1. Preheat the oven to 150°C/300°F/Gas Mark 2. Line a baking sheet with non-stick baking paper and set aside.

2. Place the baking powder, flours, sugar, cacao powder and cinnamon in a large bowl and stir together.

3. Add the eggs to the bowl and stir into the dry ingredients, adding the almonds once the dough starts coming together.

4. Turn the dough out to a floured work surface and roll it into a long sausage shape, about 35 cm/14 inches long and 6–7 cm/2½–2¾ inches wide. Place on the prepared baking sheet and bake in the preheated oven for 30–40 minutes.

5. Remove the sheet from the oven and cool on a rack for 10 minutes.

6. Cut the dough into 1–cm/½-inch thick slices and bake for a further 8–10 minutes on each side, until firm. Cool on a rack.

7. Gently melt the dark and white chocolate in separate heatproof bowls, over pans of simmering water. Don't let the bowls touch the water. Once melted, drizzle lines of chocolate over the biscotti to decorate. Leave to set before serving.

WHY NOT TRY?
Add dried fruits, such as cranberries or chopped apricots, for extra sweetness.

PER BISCOTTI: 178 KCALS | 8.6G FAT | 2.6G SAT FAT | 22.3G CARBS | 11.7G SUGARS | 2.2G FIBRE | 4.7G PROTEIN | 0.1G SALT

RASPBERRY, CHIA SEED AND PECAN POTS

*Chia seeds may be tiny but they're packed with protein, fibre and omega-3 fats.
In addition to the health boost, they give juices and puréed fruits gorgeous texture.*

SERVES: 4
PREP: 10 MINS   COOK: NONE

400 g/14 oz raspberries
2 tbsp chia seeds
1 mango, stoned, peeled and chopped
400 g /14 oz Greek-style yogurt
3 kiwis, peeled and sliced
2 tbsp pecan nuts, toasted and roughly chopped,
to decorate

1. Place the raspberries in a food processor and blitz until smooth, then place in a bowl. Stir in the chia seeds and leave to stand – the chia seeds will gradually thicken the mixture to a jam-like consistency.

2. Place the mango in a clean processor and blitz until smooth. Lightly stir through the yogurt, leaving trails of the mango showing.

3. Layer the yogurt, raspberry-chia mixture and kiwi slices in four glasses, finishing with yogurt on top.

4. Sprinkle the pudding with chopped pecan nuts to serve.

AMAZING MANGO
A mango is 14 per cent natural sugar, and this can be quickly converted into energy by the body. It is also rich in beta-carotene and vitamin C.

PER SERVING: 281 KCALS | 10.8G FAT | 4.1G SAT FAT | 37.7G CARBS | 23.2G SUGARS | 11.8G FIBRE | 12.8G PROTEIN | 0.1G SALT

TOFU LEMON CHEESECAKE

Fibre-filled dates and naturally sweet agave syrup add flavour and appeal to the crunchy ginger biscuit base, then zesty lemons add the finest refreshing flavour to the topping of this top-notch chilled cheesecake.

SERVES: 10
PREP: 30–35 MINS, PLUS CHILLING   COOK: 5 MINS

BASE
125 g/4½ oz pecan nuts
175 g/6 oz soft dried dates
85 g/3 oz gingernut biscuits
2 tbsp agave syrup
1 tbsp lemon zest, to decorate

FILLING
350 g/12 oz firm silken tofu
300 g/10½ oz full-fat cream cheese
100 g/3½ oz Greek-style natural yogurt
juice and grated zest of 3 lemons
100 g/3½ oz soft light brown sugar
½ tsp vanilla extract
15 g/½ oz powdered gelatine
75 ml/2½ fl oz cold water

1. Line a 20-cm/8-inch round springform baking tin with baking paper.

2. To make the base, place the pecans, dates, biscuits and agave syrup in a food processor and pulse until the mixture comes together. The mixture should be slightly sticky when rolled in your hands. Empty the crust into the bottom of your prepared tin and press down to create an even base.

3. To make the filling, drain any excess water from the tofu and place in a food processor with the cream cheese, yogurt, lemon juice, lemon zest, brown sugar and vanilla extract. Blend until silky smooth.

4. Place the powdered gelatine in a small bowl and pour over the cold water. Set the bowl over a saucepan full of gently simmering water. Stir the gelatine until it has dissolved into the liquid and, working quickly, pour the liquid gelatine into the filling mixture. Blend the filling again until the gelatine is fully incorporated.

5. Spoon the filling on top of the base and place in the refrigerator to chill for 6 hours or overnight. Serve in slices, decorated with lemon zest.

PER SERVING: 368 KCALS | 22.2G FAT | 7.7G SAT FAT | 37.6G CARBS | 29.7G SUGARS | 2.9G FIBRE | 8.4G PROTEIN | 0.4G SALT

PEANUT BUTTER AND BANANA MUFFINS

These lovely muffins are healthier than most shop-bought ones and can be eaten as a guilt-free dessert after dinner or taken to work for an easy breakfast.

MAKES: 12 MUFFINS
PREP: 12 MINS   COOK: 15–20 MINS

200 g/7 oz self-raising flour
50 g/1³/₄ oz buckwheat flour
75 g /2³/₄ oz golden caster sugar
30 g/1 oz rolled oats
2 bananas, peeled and mashed
100 g/3¹/₂ oz crunchy peanut butter
2 eggs, beaten
30 g/1 oz coconut oil, melted
125 ml/4 fl oz milk

1. Preheat the oven to 200°C/400°F/Gas Mark 6. Line a 12–hole muffin tin with paper cases and set aside.

2. Sieve the flours and sugar into a large bowl, then mix in the oats.

3. In a separate bowl, mix the mashed banana and peanut butter with the eggs, melted coconut oil and milk.

4. Stir the banana mixture into the flour mixture, but do not over-mix. The tastiest muffins are made from the lumpiest batter.

5. Spoon the batter into the prepared muffin cases and bake for 15–18 minutes in the preheated oven, until risen and golden.

COOK'S TIP
Almond butter, or other nut butters, can also be used in this recipe.

PER MUFFIN: 214 KCALS | 8.3G FAT | 3.2G SAT FAT | 30.1G CARBS | 10.1G SUGARS | 2.3G FIBRE | 6.1G PROTEIN | 0.6G SALT

CHOCOLATE ORANGE MUG CAKE

There are times when all you want is some instant gratification, so here's a cake made in less than 10 minutes, with a tasty chocolate and orange sponge and almond butter for protein!

SERVES: 1
PREP: 3 MINS   COOK: 2 MINS

20 g/¾ oz almond butter
1 heaped tbsp gram flour
1 heaped tbsp cocoa powder
½ tsp baking powder
2 tsp caster sugar
1 large egg
grated zest of 1 orange
1 tbsp Greek-style yogurt, to serve

1. Place all the ingredients, except half the orange zest and the yogurt, in a large microwave-proof mug and mix together well with a teaspoon.

2. Bake in the microwave for 2 minutes, until risen and cooked through.

3. Serve the mug cake with a dollop of yogurt and a sprinkling of orange zest.

MIX IT UP
Use the basic recipe and add your own choice of flavours – chopped banana or mango work well.

PER SERVING: 361 KCALS | 20.2G FAT | 4.5G SAT FAT | 31.5G CARBS | 12.7G SUGARS | 7.9G FIBRE | 19.6G PROTEIN | 0.9G SALT

INDEX